GRAPHIC HISTORY

THE STORY OF THE STAR★SPANGLED BANNER

by Ryan Jacobson

illustrated by Cynthia Martin and
Terry Beatty

Consultant: Don Hickey, professor
Department of History
Wayne State College
Wayne, Nebraska

Capstone press

Mankato, Minnesota

Graphic Library is published by Capstone Press,
1710 Roe Crest Drive, North Mankato, Minnesota 56003.
www.capstonepub.com

 Books published by Capstone Press are manufactured with paper
containing at least 10 percent post-consumer waste.

Library of Congress Cataloging-in-Publication Data
Jacobson, Ryan.
  The story of the Star-Spangled Banner / by Ryan Jacobson; illustrated by Cynthia Martin and Terry Beatty.
    p. cm.—(Graphic library. Graphic history)
  Summary: "In graphic novel format, discusses the events leading up to the Battle of Fort McHenry
and Francis Scott Key's writing of the Star-Spangled Banner, and later how it became our national
anthem"—Provided by publisher.
  Includes bibliographical references and index.
  ISBN-13: 978-0-7368-5493-1 (hardcover)
  ISBN-10: 0-7368-5493-2 (hardcover)
  ISBN-13: 978-0-7368-6881-5 (softcover pbk.)
  ISBN-10: 0-7368-6881-X (softcover pbk.)
  1. Baltimore, Battle of, Baltimore, Md., 1814—Juvenile literature. 2. United States—History—War
of 1812—Flags—Juvenile literature. 3. Flags—United States—History—19th century—Juvenile literature.
4. Key, Francis Scott, 1779–1843—Juvenile literature. 5. Star-spangled banner (Song)—Juvenile literature.
I. Martin, Cynthia, 1961– ill. II. Terry Beatty, ill. III. Title. IV. Series.
E356.B2J33 2006
973.5'230975271—dc22   2005029448

Art Direction
Bob Lentz

Designers
Bob Lentz and Renée T. Doyle

Storyboard Artist
Juliette Peters

Production Designer
Alison Thiele

Colorist
Melissa Kaercher

Editor
Sarah L. Schuette

Editor's note: Direct quotations from primary sources are indicated by a yellow background.

Direct quotations appear on the following pages:
Page 5, from *The Dawn's Early Light* by Walter Lord (New York: Norton, 1972).
Page 14, from *The Burning of Washington: The British Invasion of 1814* by Anthony Pitch
    (Annapolis, Md.: Naval Institute Press, 1999).
Page 23, from *The Darkest Day: 1814; The Washington-Baltimore Campaign* by Charles
    Geoffrey Muller (Philadelphia: Lippincott, 1963).

Printed in the United States of America in Stevens Point, Wisconsin.
010555R

Table of Contents

Chapter 1
America at War

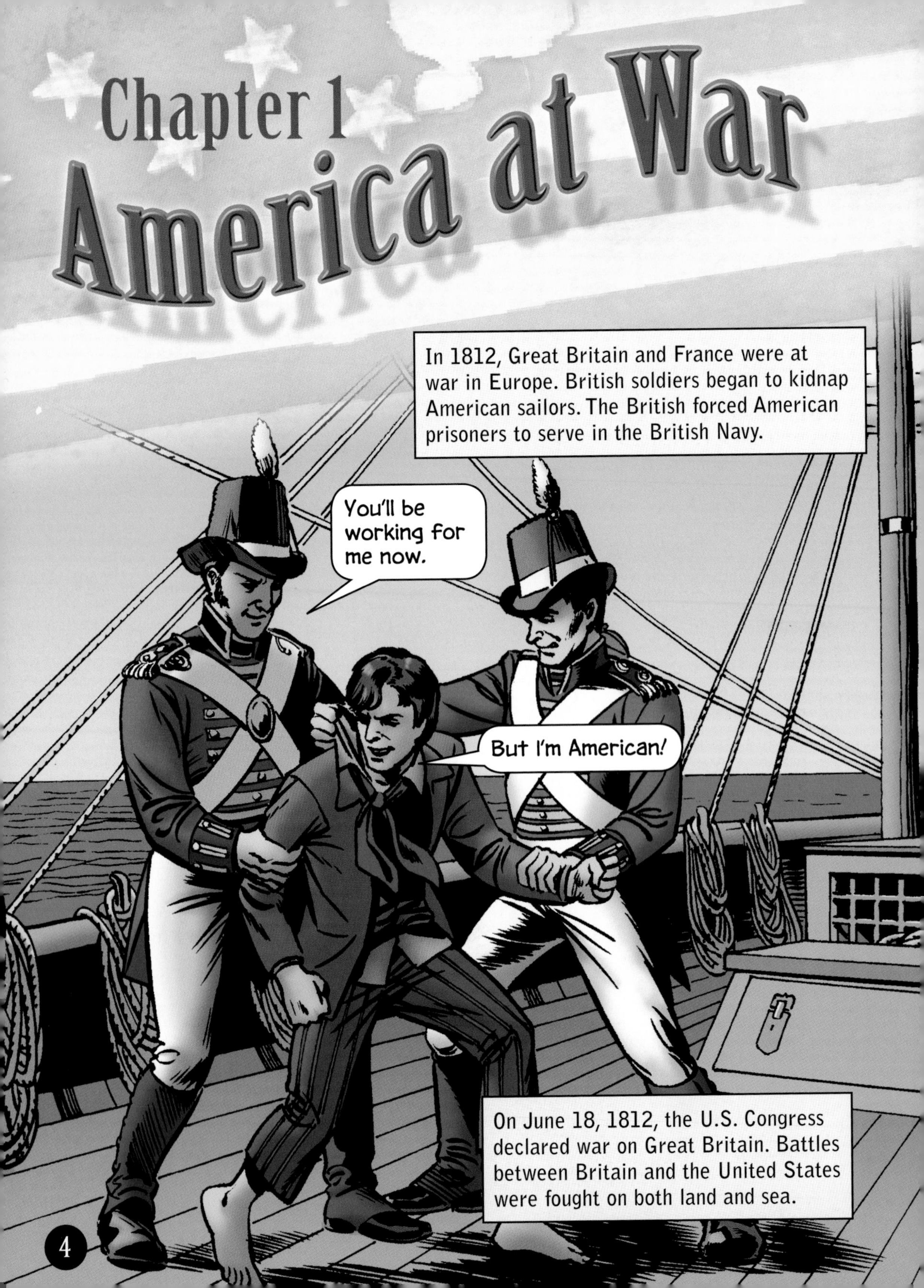
In 1812, Great Britain and France were at war in Europe. British soldiers began to kidnap American sailors. The British forced American prisoners to serve in the British Navy.
You'll be working for me now.
But I'm American!
On June 18, 1812, the U.S. Congress declared war on Great Britain. Battles between Britain and the United States were fought on both land and sea.

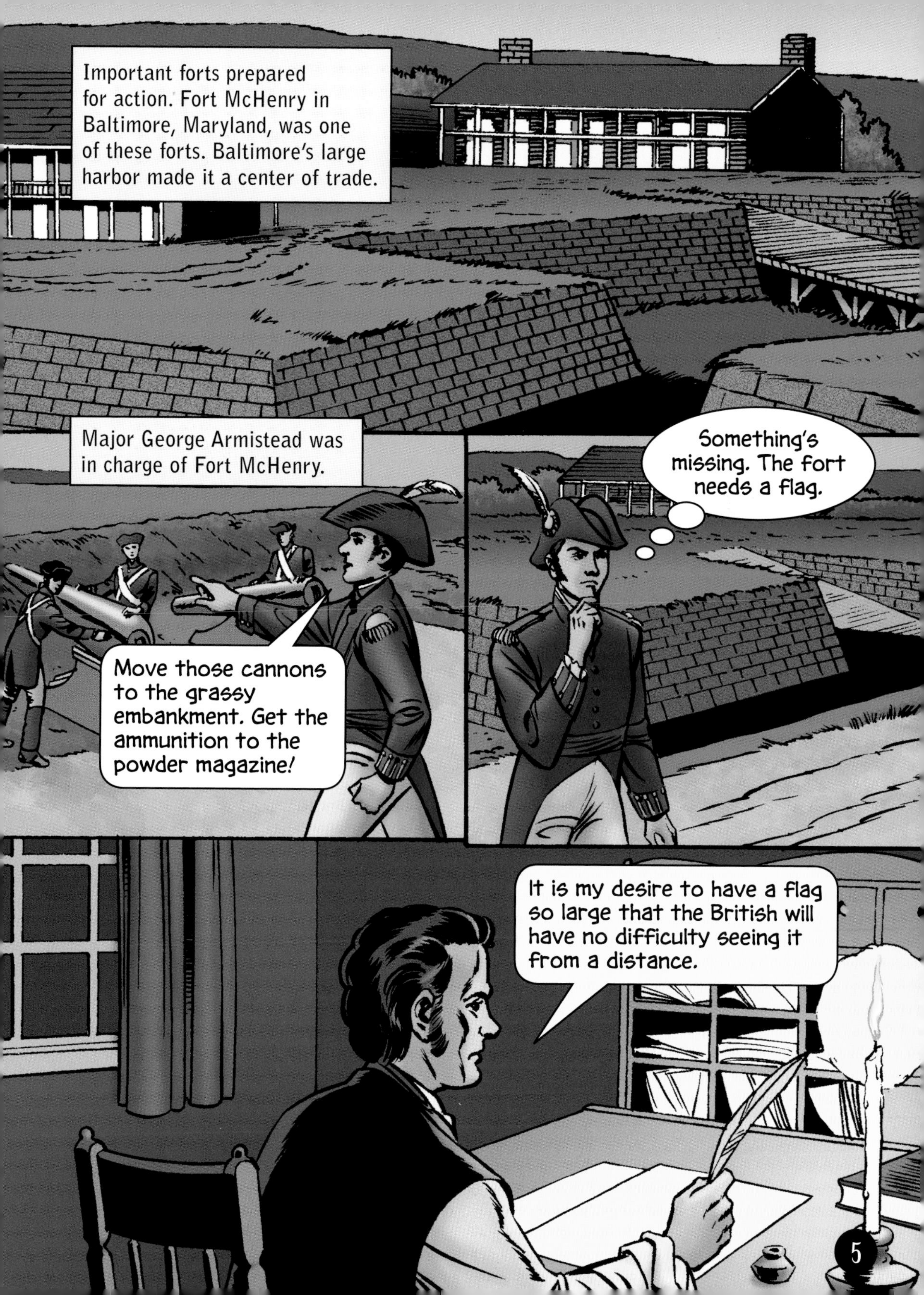
Important forts prepared for action. Fort McHenry in Baltimore, Maryland, was one of these forts. Baltimore's large harbor made it a center of trade.
Major George Armistead was in charge of Fort McHenry.
Move those cannons to the grassy embankment. Get the ammunition to the powder magazine!
Something's missing. The fort needs a flag.
It is my desire to have a flag so large that the British will have no difficulty seeing it from a distance.

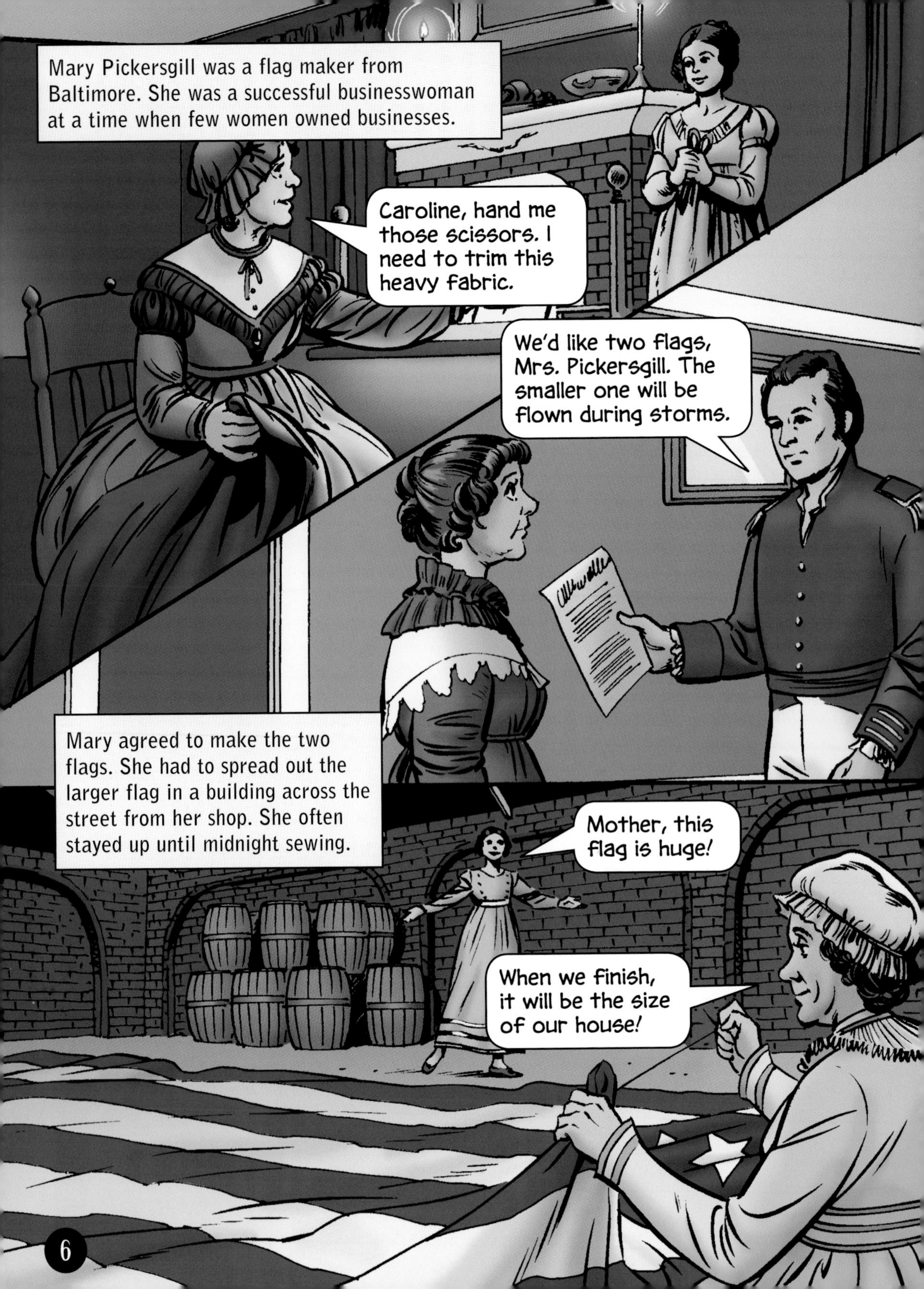

Mary Pickersgill was a flag maker from Baltimore. She was a successful businesswoman at a time when few women owned businesses.
Caroline, hand me those scissors. I need to trim this heavy fabric.
We'd like two flags, Mrs. Pickersgill. The smaller one will be flown during storms.
Mary agreed to make the two flags. She had to spread out the larger flag in a building across the street from her shop. She often stayed up until midnight sewing.
Mother, this flag is huge!
When we finish, it will be the size of our house!

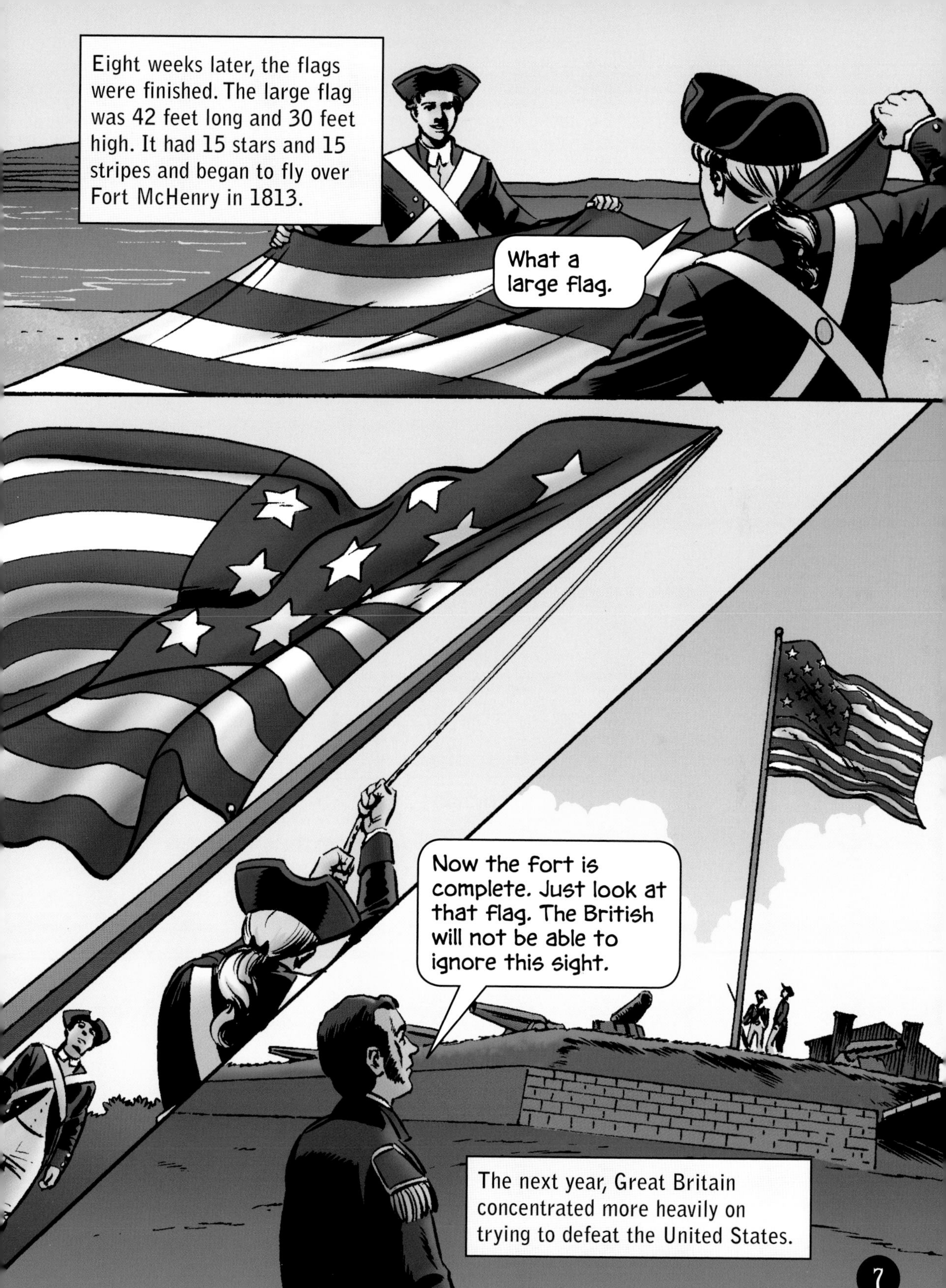
Eight weeks later, the flags were finished. The large flag was 42 feet long and 30 feet high. It had 15 stars and 15 stripes and began to fly over Fort McHenry in 1813.
What a large flag.
Now the fort is complete. Just look at that flag. The British will not be able to ignore this sight.
The next year, Great Britain concentrated more heavily on trying to defeat the United States.

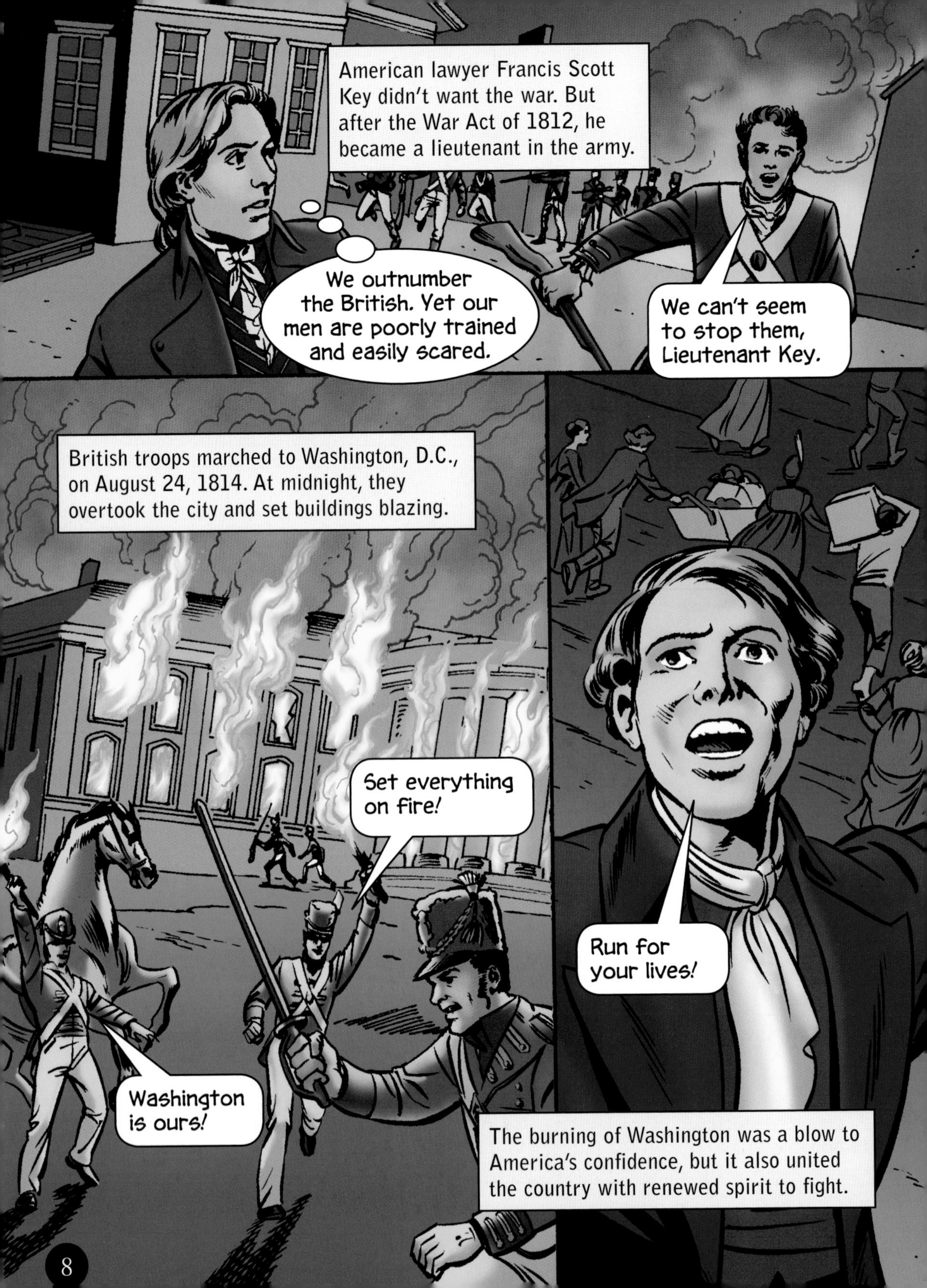
American lawyer Francis Scott Key didn't want the war. But after the War Act of 1812, he became a lieutenant in the army.
We outnumber the British. Yet our men are poorly trained and easily scared.
We can't seem to stop them, Lieutenant Key.
British troops marched to Washington, D.C., on August 24, 1814. At midnight, they overtook the city and set buildings blazing.
Set everything on fire!
Washington is ours!
Run for your lives!
The burning of Washington was a blow to America's confidence, but it also united the country with renewed spirit to fight.

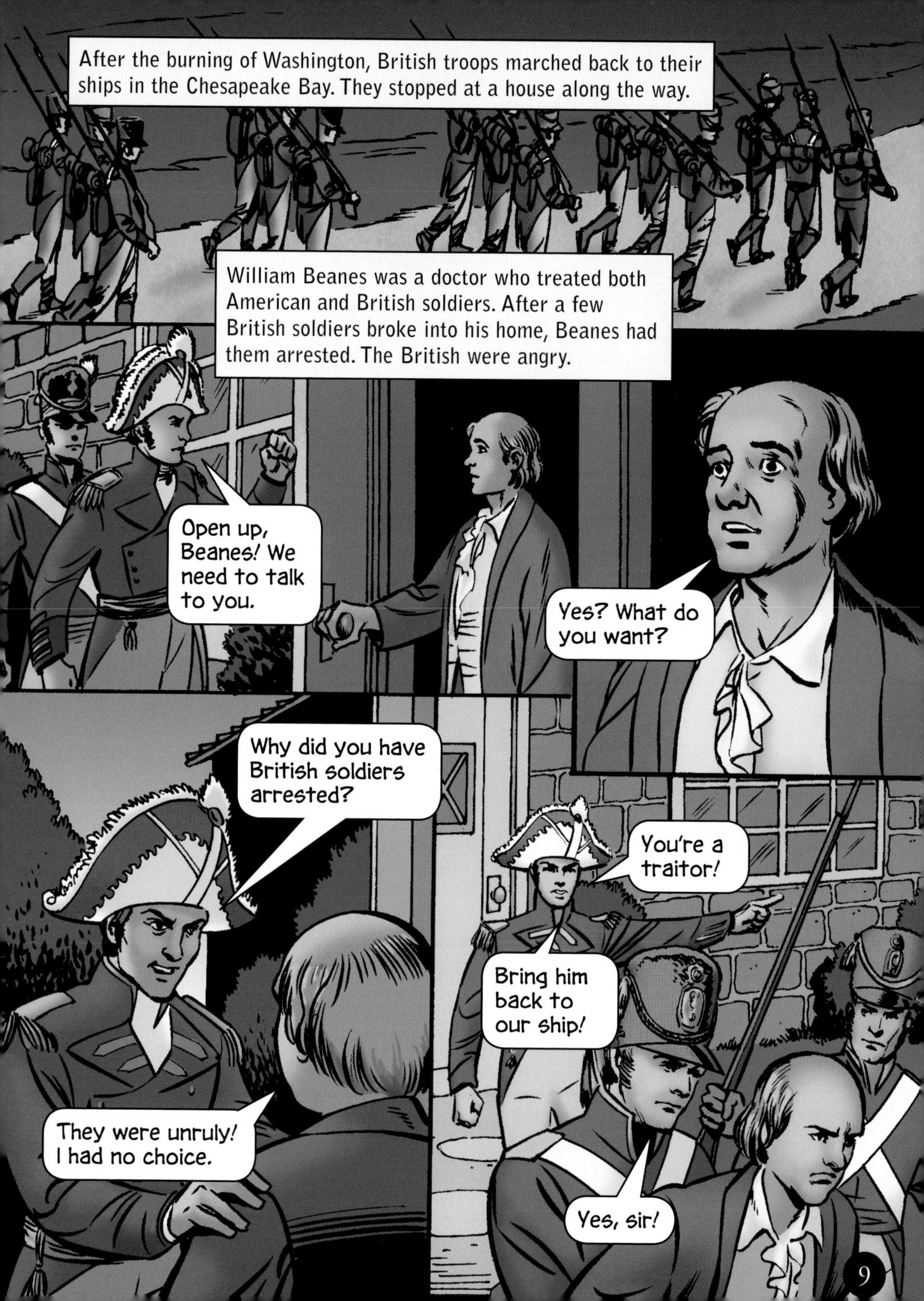
After the burning of Washington, British troops marched back to their ships in the Chesapeake Bay. They stopped at a house along the way.
William Beanes was a doctor who treated both American and British soldiers. After a few British soldiers broke into his home, Beanes had them arrested. The British were angry.
Open up, Beanes! We need to talk to you.
Yes? What do you want?
Why did you have British soldiers arrested?
They were unruly! I had no choice.
You're a traitor!
Bring him back to our ship!
Yes, sir!

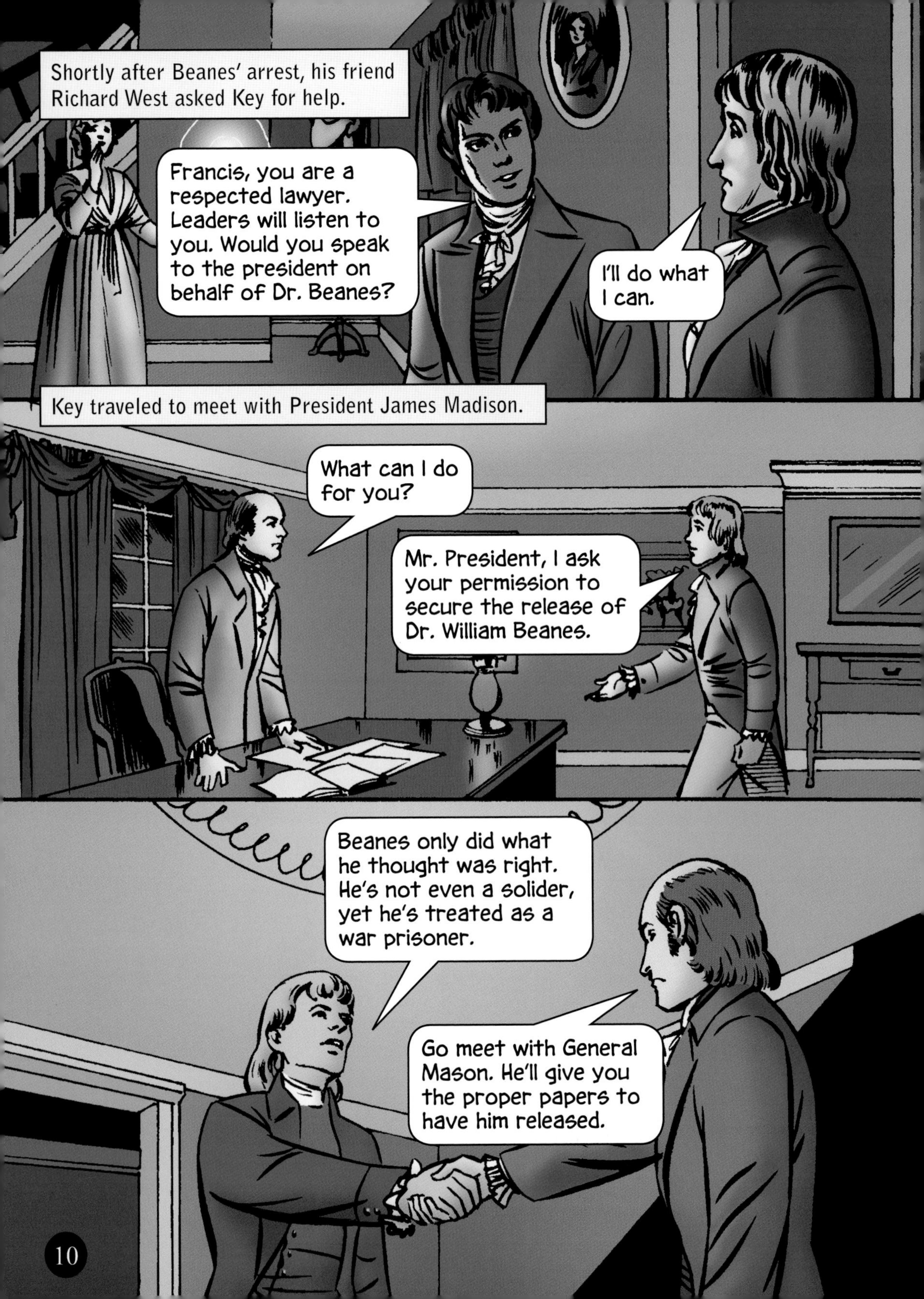

Shortly after Beanes' arrest, his friend Richard West asked Key for help.
Francis, you are a respected lawyer. Leaders will listen to you. Would you speak to the president on behalf of Dr. Beanes?
I'll do what I can.
Key traveled to meet with President James Madison.
What can I do for you?
Mr. President, I ask your permission to secure the release of Dr. William Beanes.
Beanes only did what he thought was right. He's not even a solider, yet he's treated as a war prisoner.
Go meet with General Mason. He'll give you the proper papers to have him released.

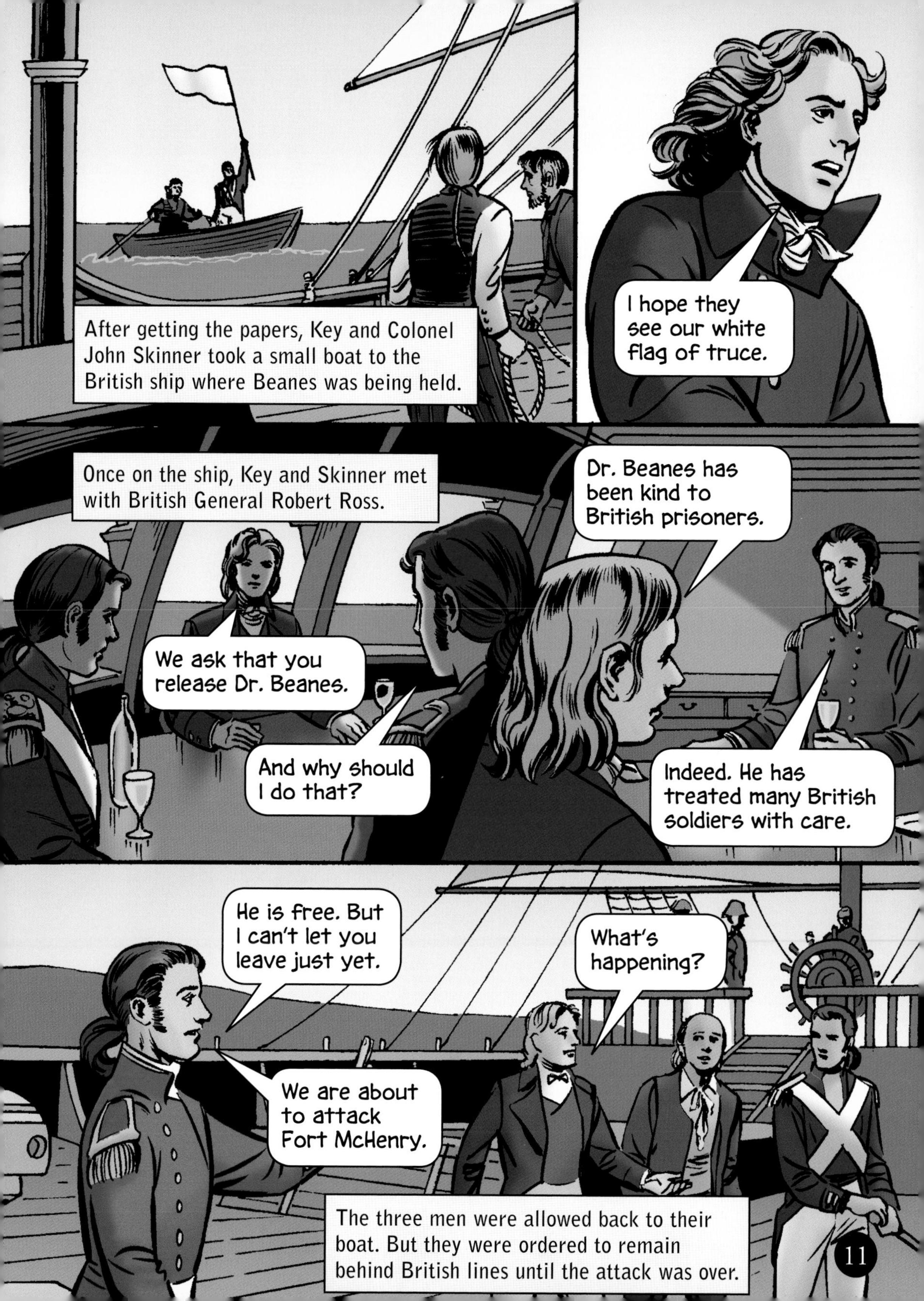
After getting the papers, Key and Colonel John Skinner took a small boat to the British ship where Beanes was being held.
I hope they see our white flag of truce.
Once on the ship, Key and Skinner met with British General Robert Ross.
We ask that you release Dr. Beanes.
And why should I do that?
Dr. Beanes has been kind to British prisoners.
Indeed. He has treated many British soldiers with care.
He is free. But I can't let you leave just yet.
We are about to attack Fort McHenry.
What's happening?
The three men were allowed back to their boat. But they were ordered to remain behind British lines until the attack was over.

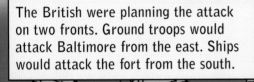

Chapter 2
Defending Fort McHenry

The British were planning the attack on two fronts. Ground troops would attack Baltimore from the east. Ships would attack the fort from the south.

Meanwhile, at Fort McHenry, Armistead tried to ready his soldiers.

Prepare the fort for battle, men.

Yes, sir!

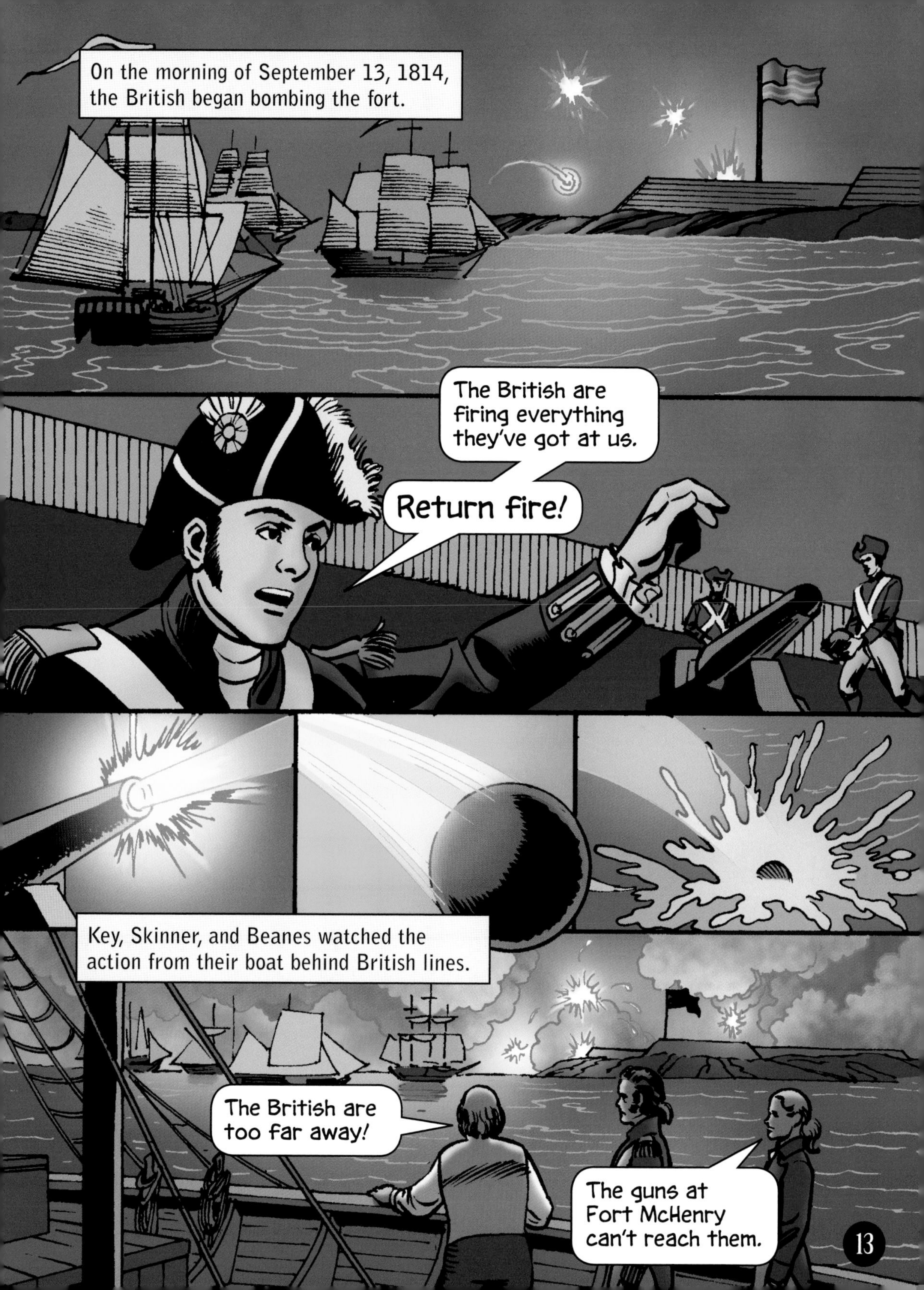
On the morning of September 13, 1814, the British began bombing the fort.
The British are firing everything they've got at us.
Return fire!
Key, Skinner, and Beanes watched the action from their boat behind British lines.
The British are too far away!
The guns at Fort McHenry can't reach them.

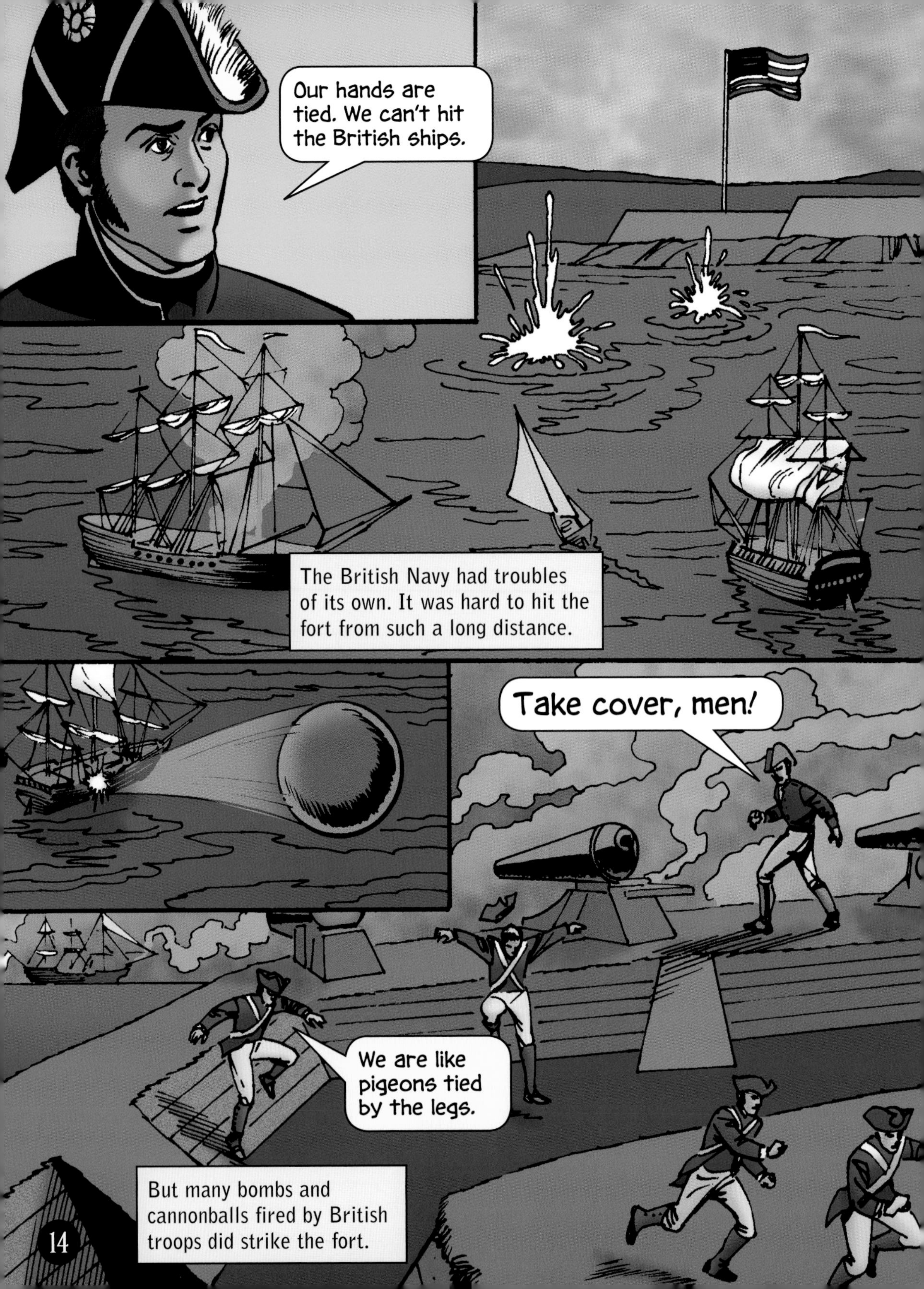
Our hands are tied. We can't hit the British ships.
The British Navy had troubles of its own. It was hard to hit the fort from such a long distance.
Take cover, men!
We are like pigeons tied by the legs.
But many bombs and cannonballs fired by British troops did strike the fort.

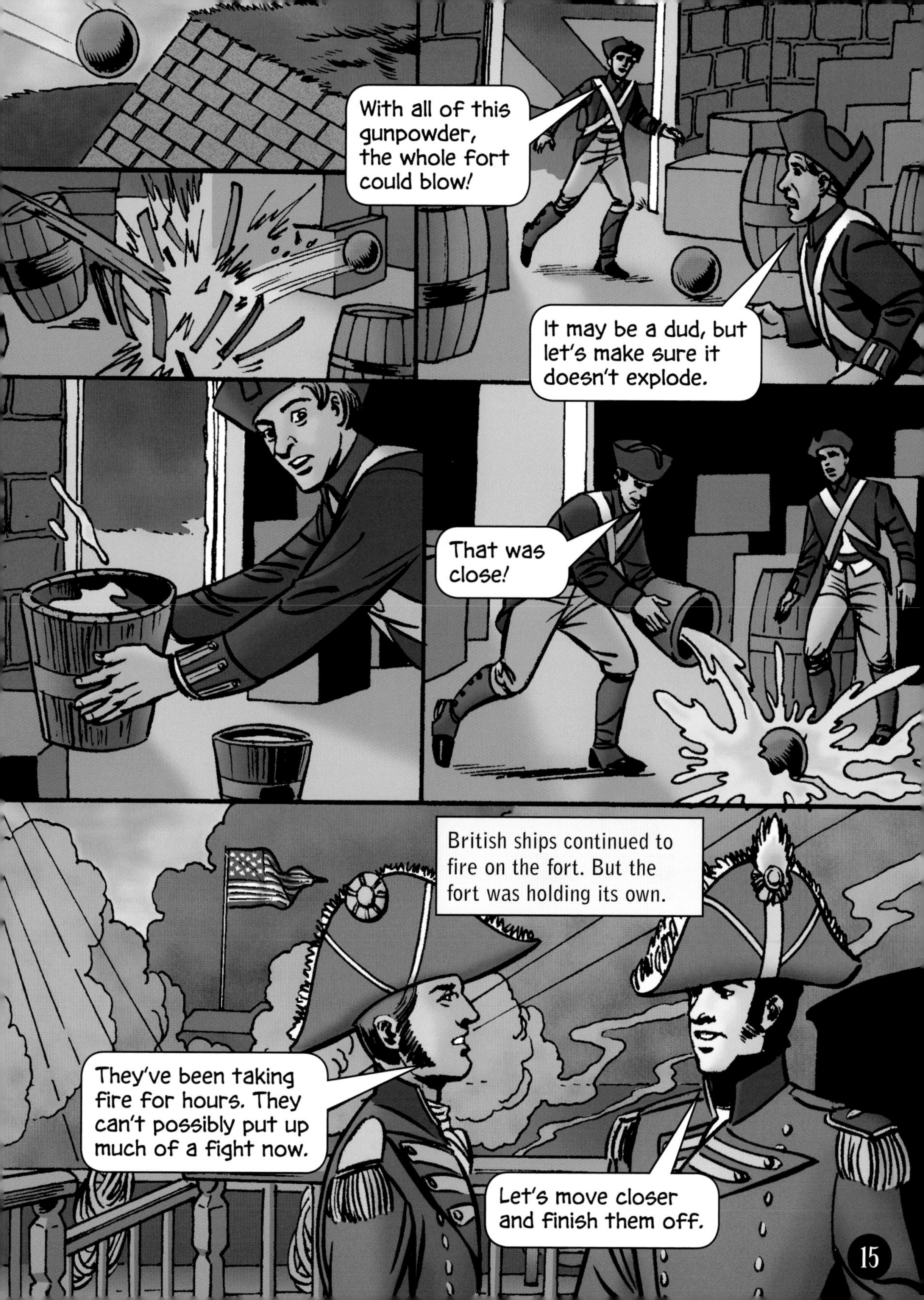

With all of this gunpowder, the whole fort could blow!
It may be a dud, but let's make sure it doesn't explode.
That was close!
British ships continued to fire on the fort. But the fort was holding its own.
They've been taking fire for hours. They can't possibly put up much of a fight now.
Let's move closer and finish them off.

Chapter 3
A Long, Dark Night

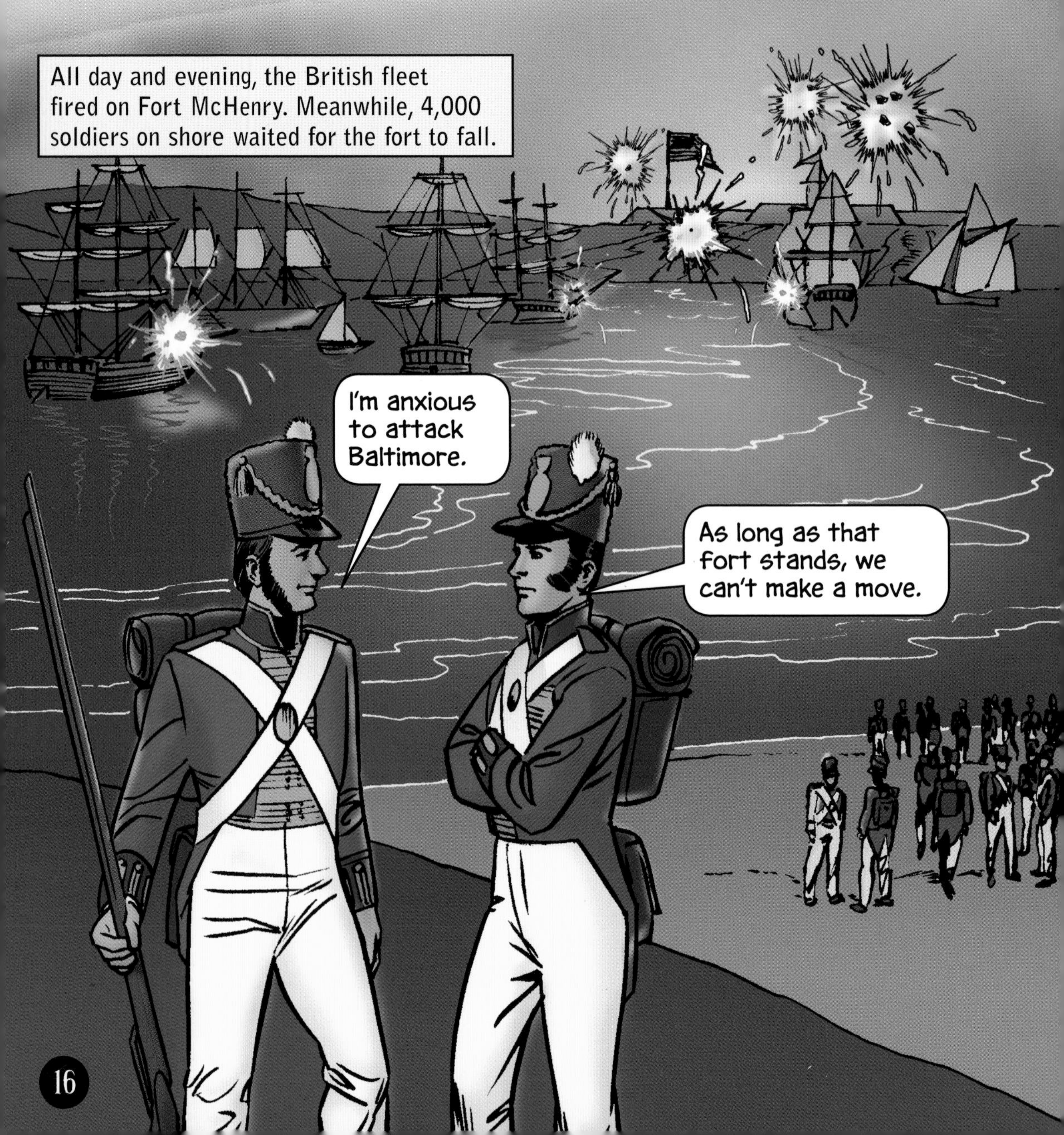
All day and evening, the British fleet fired on Fort McHenry. Meanwhile, 4,000 soldiers on shore waited for the fort to fall.
I'm anxious to attack Baltimore.
As long as that fort stands, we can't make a move.

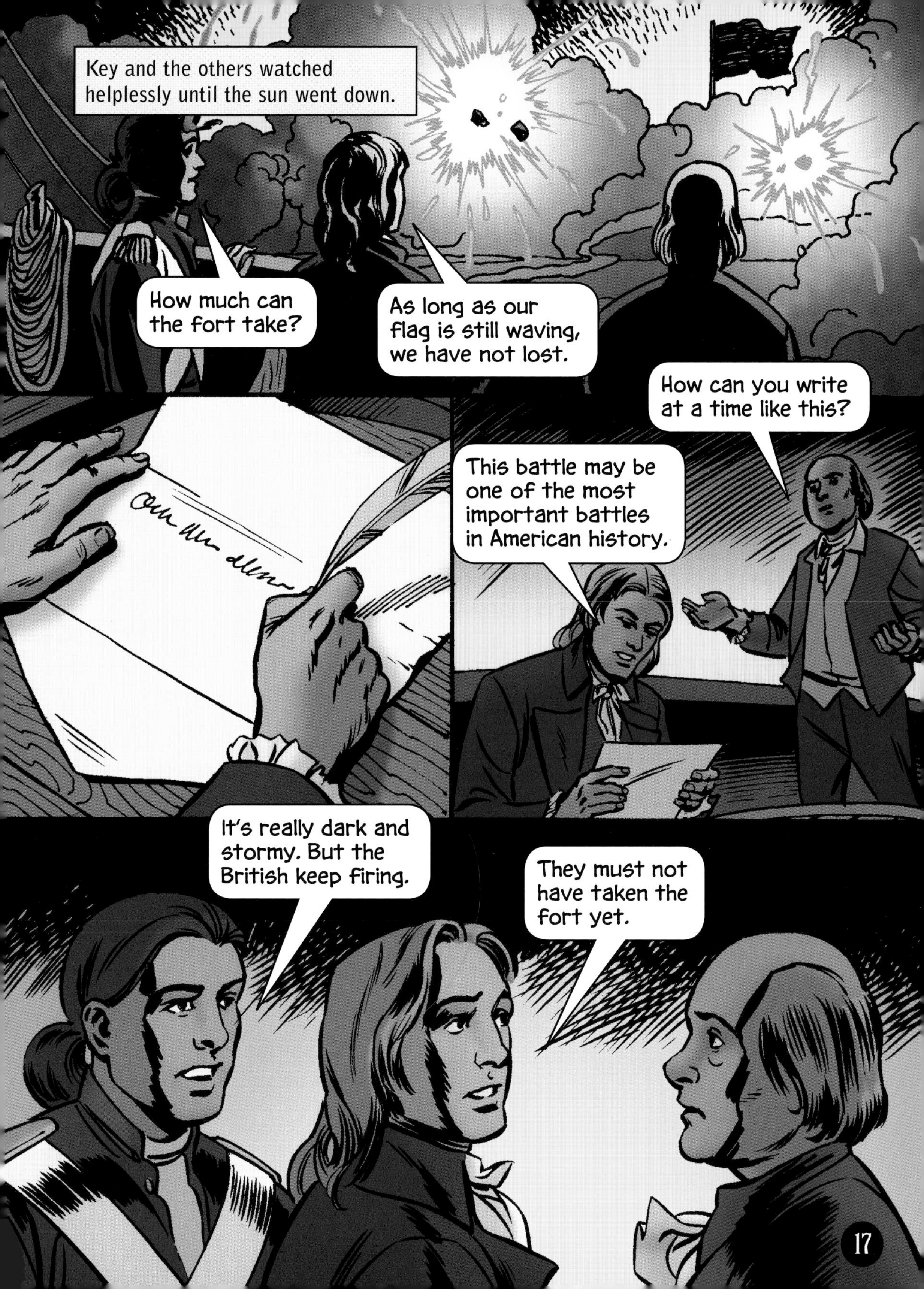
Key and the others watched helplessly until the sun went down.
How much can the fort take?
As long as our flag is still waving, we have not lost.
How can you write at a time like this?
This battle may be one of the most important battles in American history.
It's really dark and stormy. But the British keep firing.
They must not have taken the fort yet.

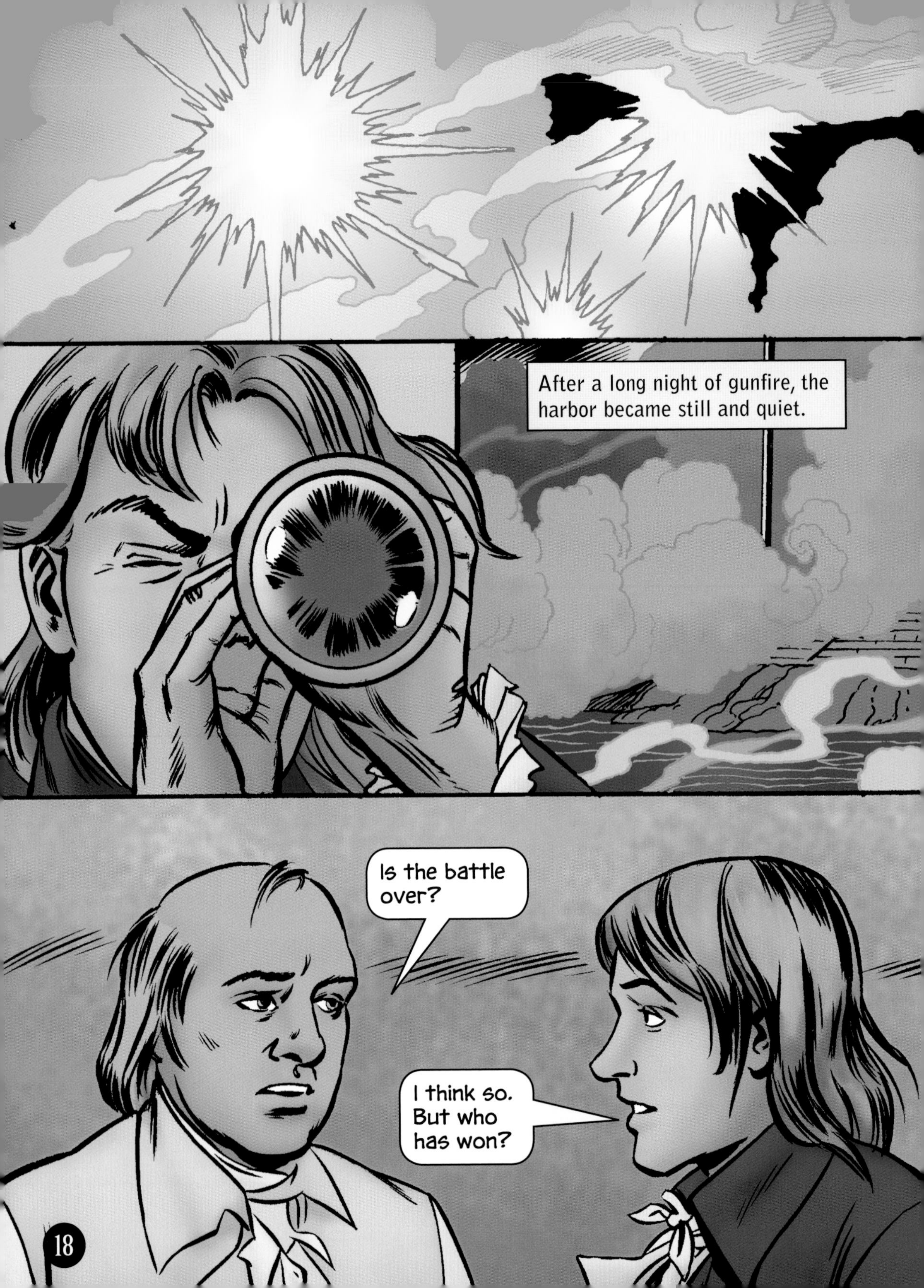
After a long night of gunfire, the harbor became still and quiet.
Is the battle over?
I think so. But who has won?

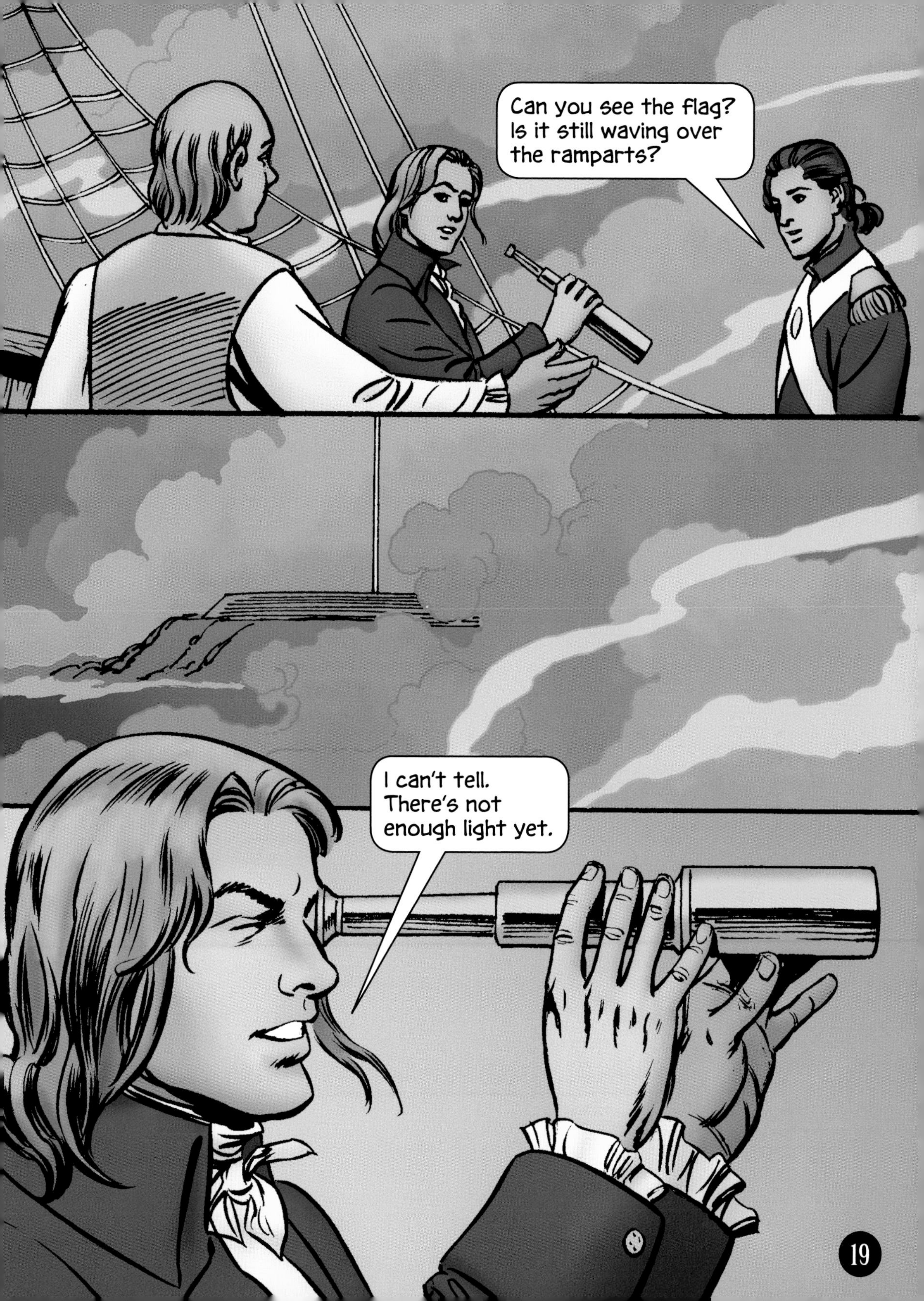
Can you see the flag? Is it still waving over the ramparts?
I can't tell. There's not enough light yet.

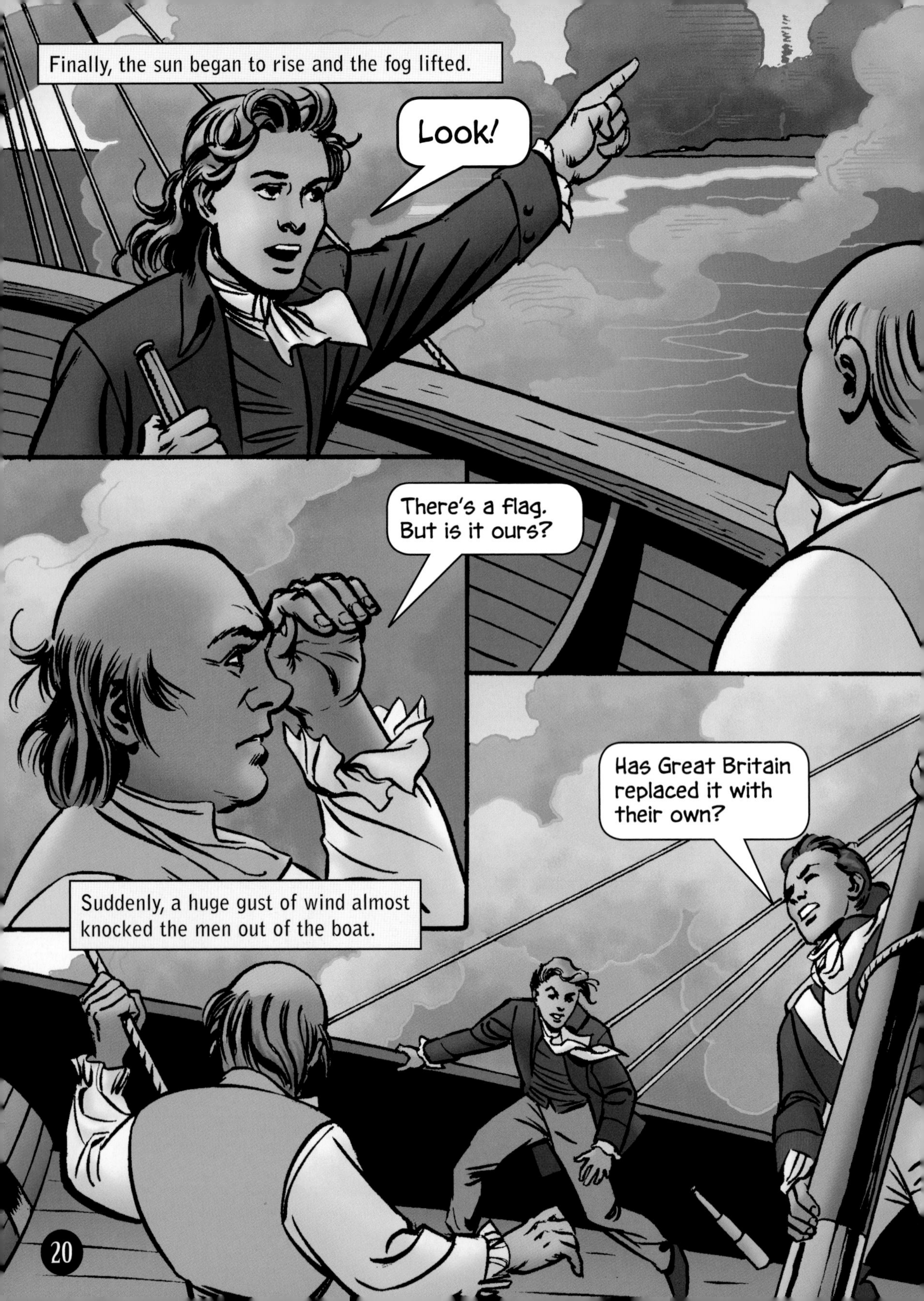
Finally, the sun began to rise and the fog lifted.
Look!
There's a flag. But is it ours?
Has Great Britain replaced it with their own?
Suddenly, a huge gust of wind almost knocked the men out of the boat.

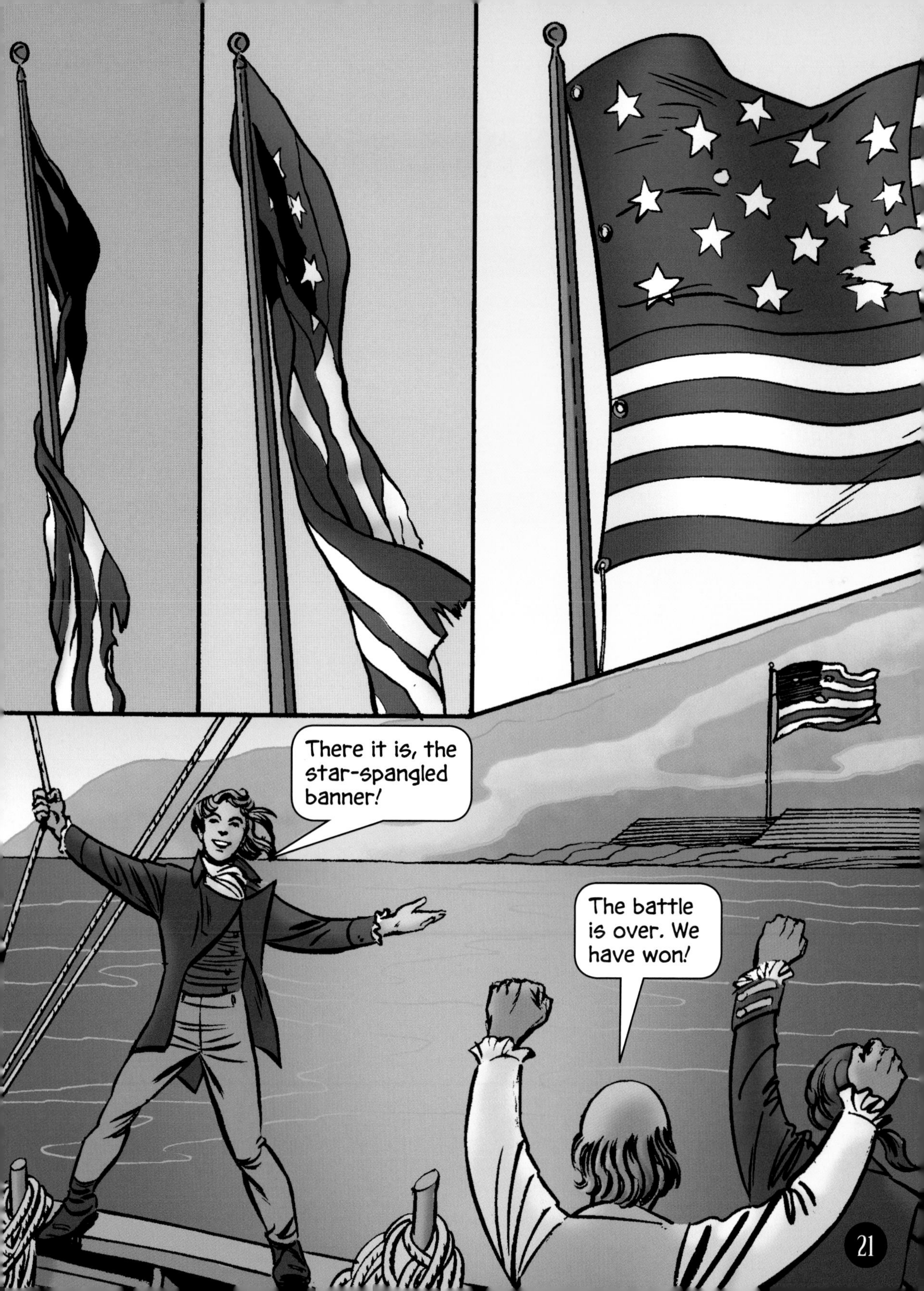
There it is, the star-spangled banner!
The battle is over. We have won!

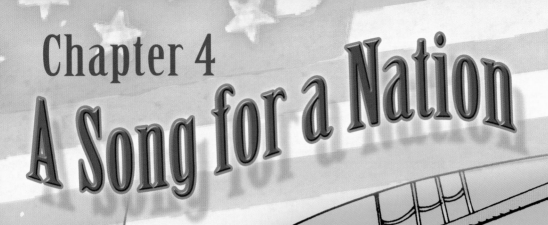

Chapter 4
A Song for a Nation

With no hope of victory, the British retreated. Beanes, Skinner, and Key sailed to Baltimore. Key continued to write about the battle on the back of an envelope.

Through the night, the flag was still there.

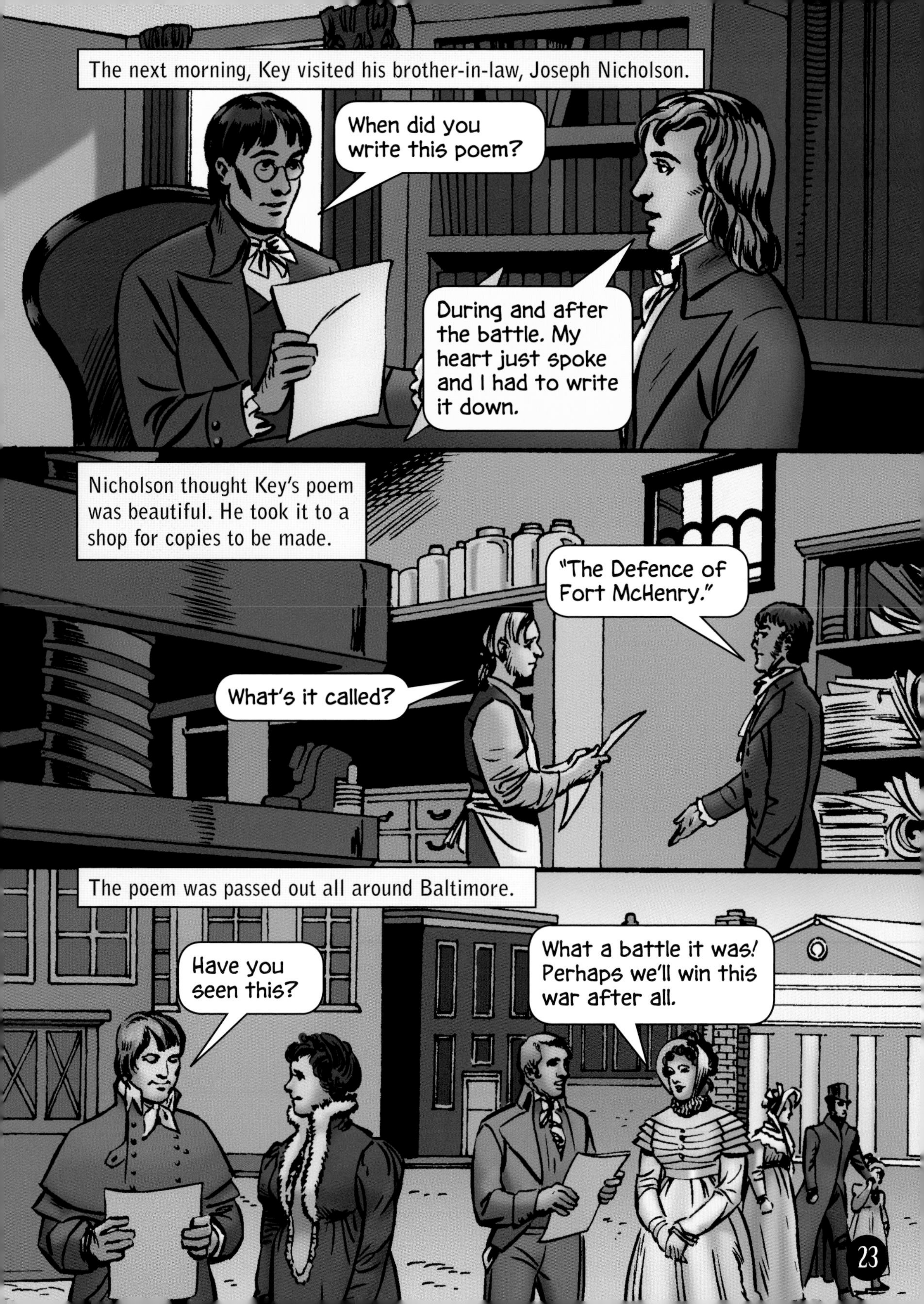
The next morning, Key visited his brother-in-law, Joseph Nicholson.
When did you write this poem?
During and after the battle. My heart just spoke and I had to write it down.
Nicholson thought Key's poem was beautiful. He took it to a shop for copies to be made.
What's it called?
"The Defence of Fort McHenry."
The poem was passed out all around Baltimore.
Have you seen this?
What a battle it was! Perhaps we'll win this war after all.

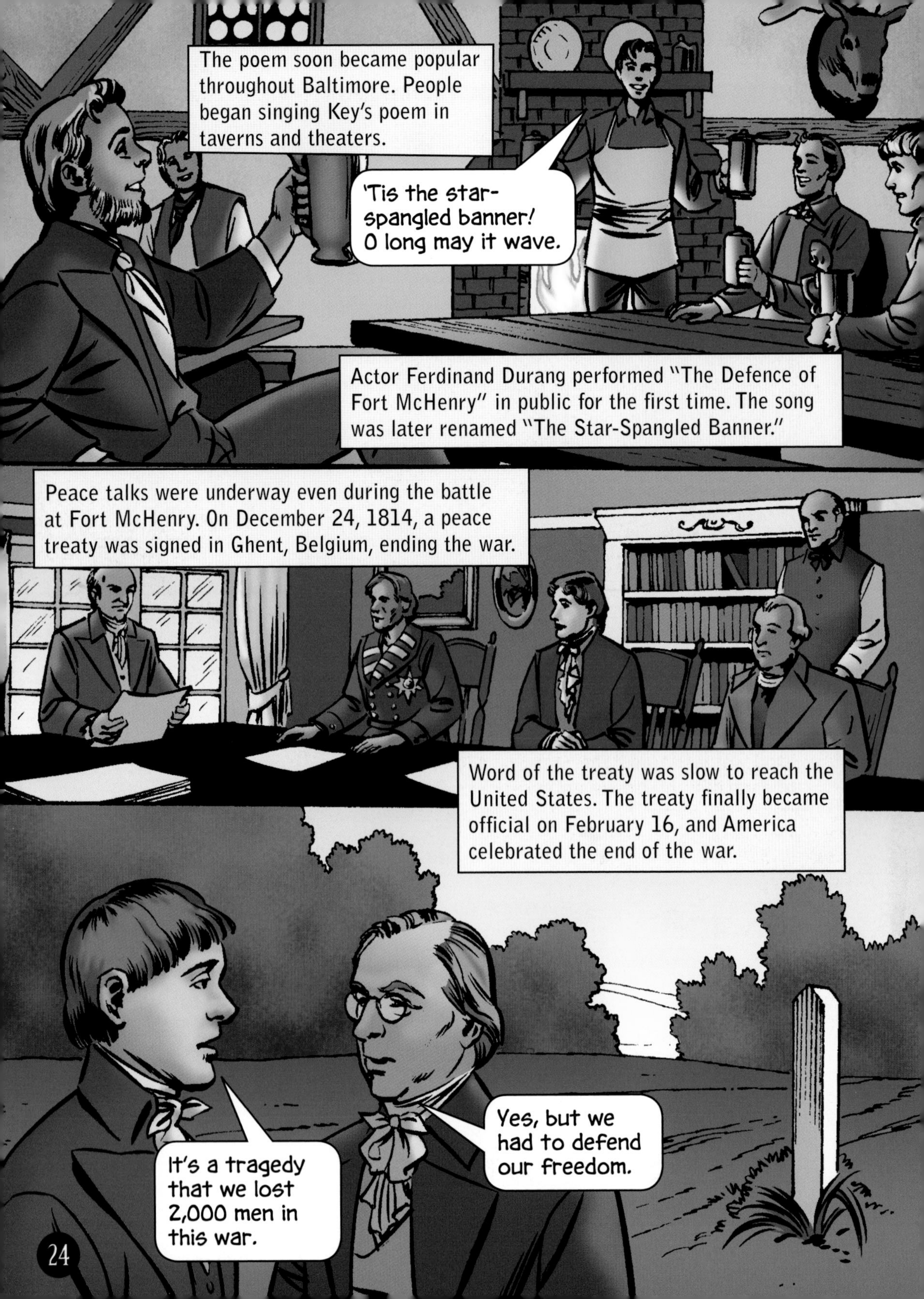
The poem soon became popular throughout Baltimore. People began singing Key's poem in taverns and theaters.
'Tis the star-spangled banner! O long may it wave.
Actor Ferdinand Durang performed "The Defence of Fort McHenry" in public for the first time. The song was later renamed "The Star-Spangled Banner."
Peace talks were underway even during the battle at Fort McHenry. On December 24, 1814, a peace treaty was signed in Ghent, Belgium, ending the war.
Word of the treaty was slow to reach the United States. The treaty finally became official on February 16, and America celebrated the end of the war.
It's a tragedy that we lost 2,000 men in this war.
Yes, but we had to defend our freedom.

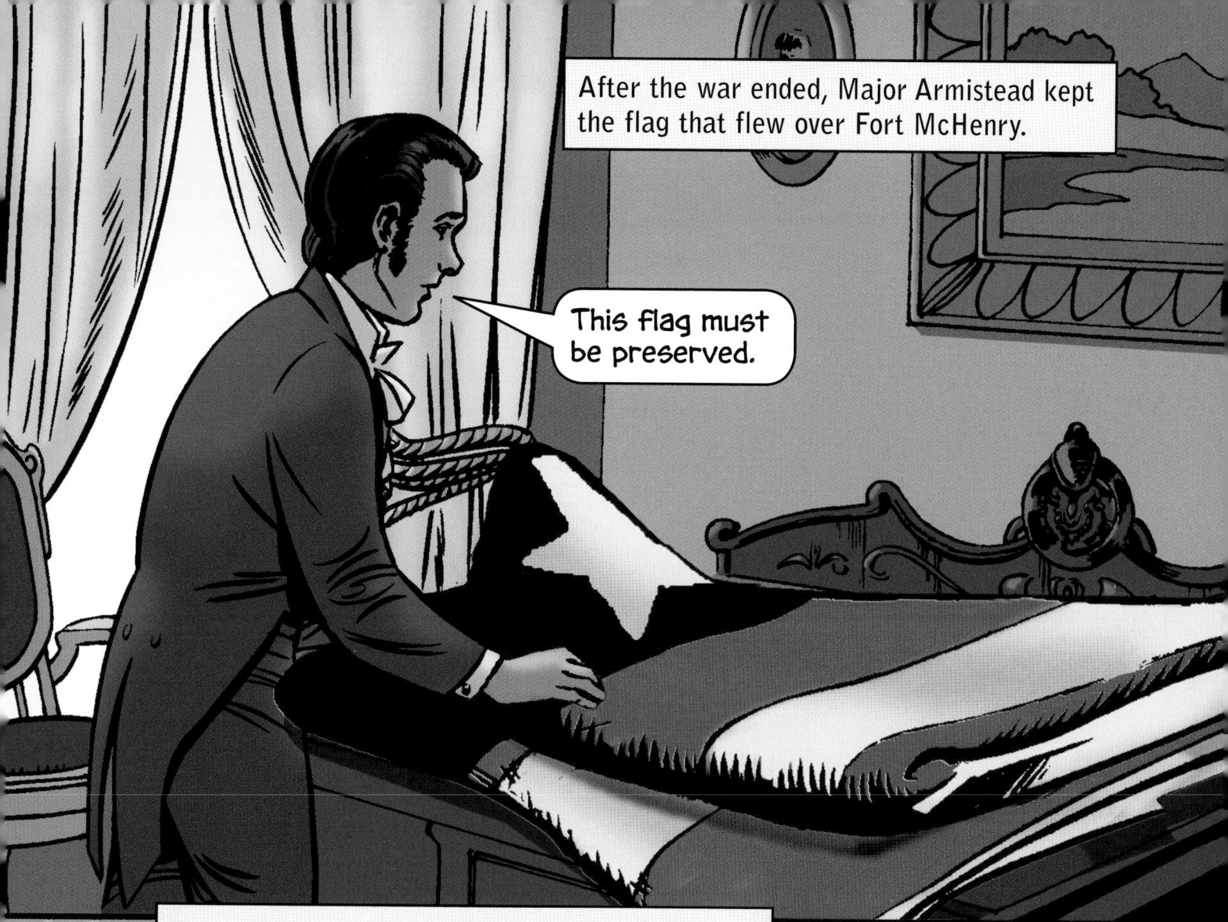
After the war ended, Major Armistead kept the flag that flew over Fort McHenry.
This flag must be preserved.

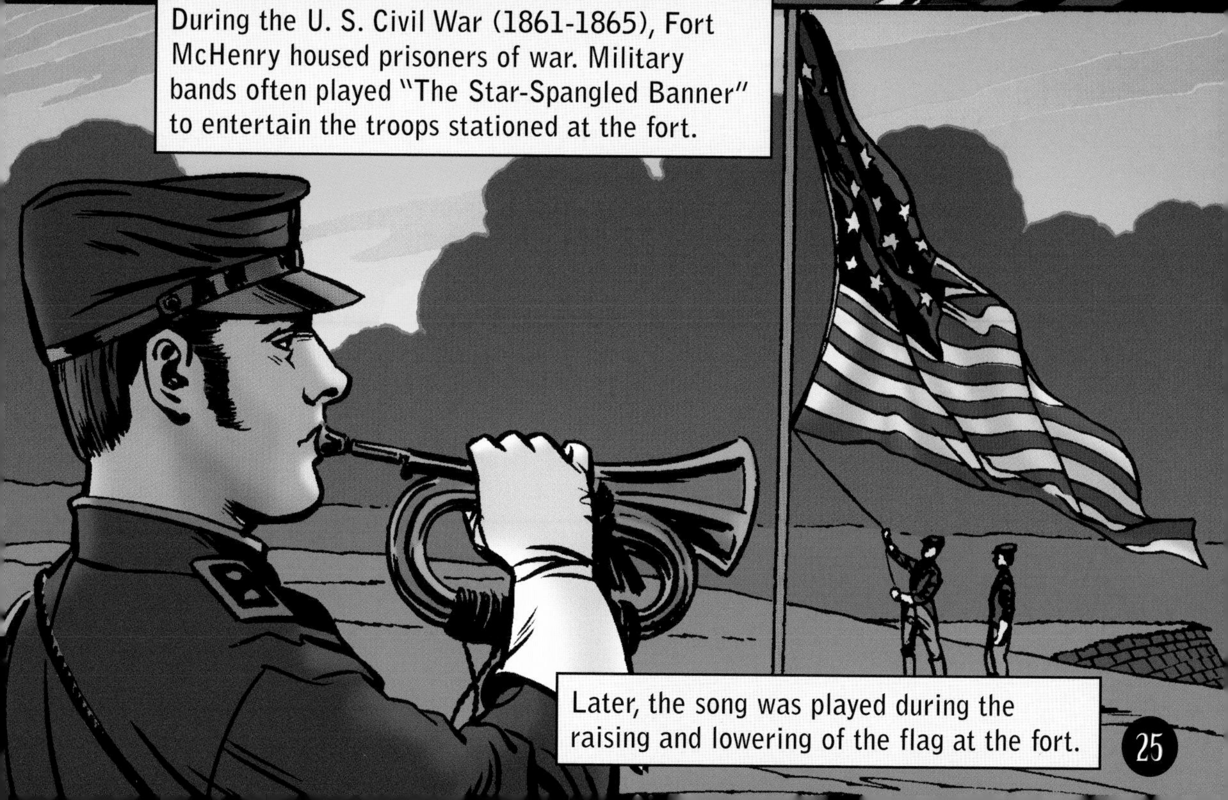
During the U. S. Civil War (1861-1865), Fort McHenry housed prisoners of war. Military bands often played "The Star-Spangled Banner" to entertain the troops stationed at the fort.
Later, the song was played during the raising and lowering of the flag at the fort.

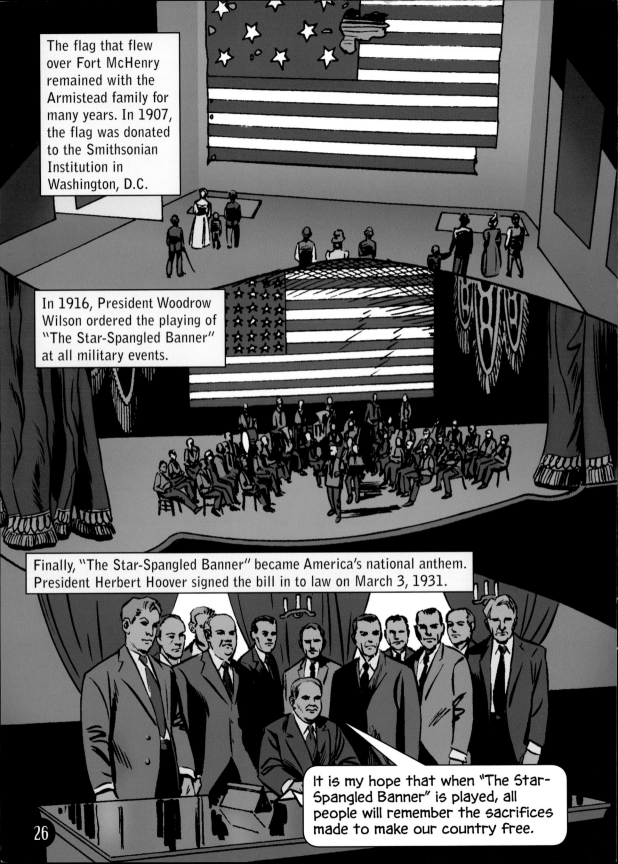

The flag that flew over Fort McHenry remained with the Armistead family for many years. In 1907, the flag was donated to the Smithsonian Institution in Washington, D.C.

In 1916, President Woodrow Wilson ordered the playing of "The Star-Spangled Banner" at all military events.

Finally, "The Star-Spangled Banner" became America's national anthem. President Herbert Hoover signed the bill in to law on March 3, 1931.

It is my hope that when "The Star-Spangled Banner" is played, all people will remember the sacrifices made to make our country free.

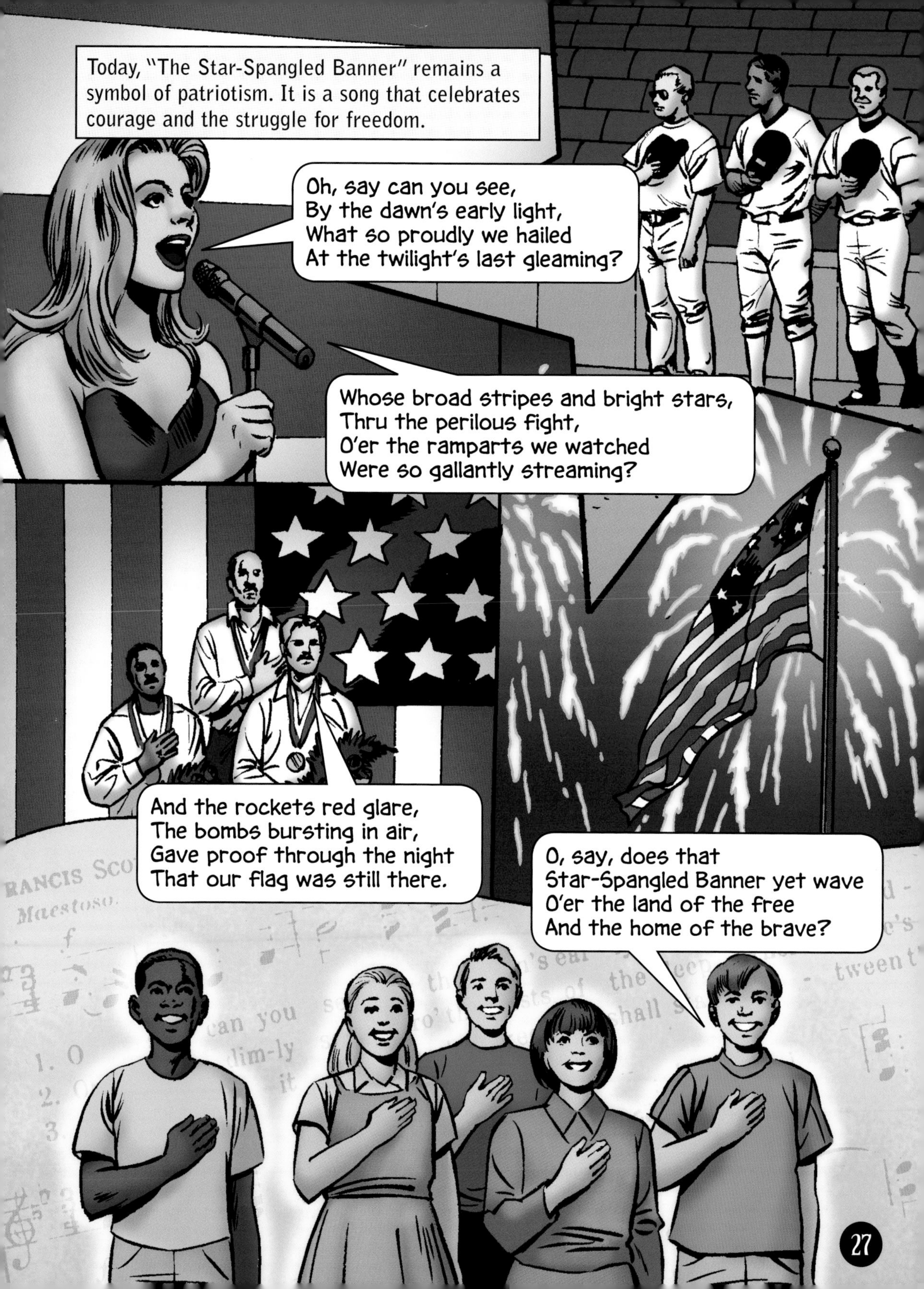
Today, "The Star-Spangled Banner" remains a symbol of patriotism. It is a song that celebrates courage and the struggle for freedom.
Oh, say can you see, By the dawn's early light, What so proudly we hailed At the twilight's last gleaming?
Whose broad stripes and bright stars, Thru the perilous fight, O'er the ramparts we watched Were so gallantly streaming?
And the rockets red glare, The bombs bursting in air, Gave proof through the night That our flag was still there.
O, say, does that Star-Spangled Banner yet wave O'er the land of the free And the home of the brave?

More about the
FLAG and the SONG

★★★★★★★★★★★★★★★★★★★

★ Fort McHenry was under fire for 25 hours. About 400 bombs exploded above the fort or fell within its outer walls. Only four Americans were killed.

★ The flag at Fort McHenry with 15 stars and 15 stripes was the second official version of the American flag. Later, the stripes were reduced to 13 to stand for the first 13 colonies, and each state was given a star.

★ Each of the stars on the flag made by Mary Pickersgill measured 2 feet from point to point. Pickersgill was paid $405.90 for her work.

★ Historians believe that the smaller flag was flown during most of the battle. The large flag was raised near the end of the battle. No one knows what happened to the small flag.

★ After his death, Armistead's widow, Louisa, allowed people to cut pieces out of the flag for keepsakes. When the flag was donated to the Smithsonian, 8 feet of material were missing.

★ Francis Scott Key suggested that "The Defence of Fort McHenry" be sung to the tune of the British song, "To Anacreon in Heaven."

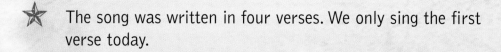 The song was written in four verses. We only sing the first verse today.

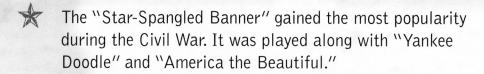 The "Star-Spangled Banner" gained the most popularity during the Civil War. It was played along with "Yankee Doodle" and "America the Beautiful."

★ When "The Star-Spangled Banner" is sung or played, most Americans stand and put their right hand over their hearts. They do it to show respect for the United States and for the flag.

★ In 1998, the Smithsonian began preserving the flag. Scientists are trying to preserve it for future generations. The process continues today.

★ Today, Fort McHenry is a National Monument and Shrine. At the fort's museum, visitors can see a cannonball that hit the fort during the Battle of Baltimore.

GLOSSARY

Congress (KONG-griss)—the branch of the U.S. government that makes laws

embankment (em-BANGK-muhnt)—a high bank at the sides of a body of water built to keep it from flooding

harbor (HAR-bur)—a place where ships load and unload passengers and cargo

powder magazine (POU-dur MAG-uh-zeen)—a building where gunpowder is stored

rampart (RAM-part)—the surrounding wall of a fort built to protect against an attack

truce (TROOSS)—a temporary agreement to stop fighting

INTERNET SITES

FactHound offers a safe, fun way to find Internet sites related to this book. All of the sites on FactHound have been researched by our staff.

Here's how:

1. *Visit www.facthound.com*
2. Type in this special code **0736854932** for age-appropriate sites. Or enter a search word related to this book for a more general search.
3. Click on the **Fetch It** button.

FactHound will fetch the best sites for you!

READ MORE

Crewe, Sabrina, and Scott Ingram. *The Writing of "The Star-Spangled Banner."* Events That Shaped America. Milwaukee: Gareth Stevens, 2005.

Dell, Pamela. *The National Anthem.* Let's See Library. Minneapolis: Compass Point Books, 2004.

Kjelle, Marylou Morano. *Francis Scott Key.* Historical Interests. Hockessin, Del.: Mitchell Lane, 2006.

BIBLIOGRAPHY

Elting, John Robert. *Amateurs to Arms! A Military History of the War of 1812.* Major Battles and Campaigns: 4. Chapel Hill, N.C.: Algonquin Books of Chapel Hill, 1991.

Lord, Walter. *The Dawn's Early Light.* New York: Norton, 1972.

Muller, Charles Geoffrey. *The Darkest Day: 1814 The Washington-Baltimore Campaign.* Great Battles of History. Philadelphia: Lippincott, 1963.

Pitch, Anthony S. *The Burning of Washington: The British Invasion of 1814.* Annapolis, Md.: Naval Institute Press, 1999.

Sheads, Scott S. *Guardian of the Star-Spangled Banner: Lt. Colonel George Armistead and the Fort McHenry Flag.* Baltimore: Toomey Press, 1999.

Taylor, Lonn. *The Star-Spangled Banner: The Flag That Inspired the National Anthem.* Washington, D.C. : National Museum of American History, Smithsonian Institution, 2000.

INDEX